Contents

What is art?. 4

What kinds of art can I do? 6

What is drawing?. 8

What can I draw with?. 10

What can I draw on? 12

What can I draw? 14

What else can I draw? 16

How does drawing make me feel? . . . 18

Let's draw! 20

Quiz 22

Glossary. 23

Index 24

Answers to quiz. 24

What is art?

Art is something you make when you are being **creative**.

People like to look at art.

Action Art

Drawing

Isabel Thomas

www.raintreepublishers.co.uk
Visit our website to find out more info

To order:
☎ Phone 44 (0) 1865 888112
🖹 Send a fax to 44 (0) 1865 314091
💻 Visit the Raintree Bookshop at **www.r**
catalogue and order online.

our

First published in Great Britain by Raintree,
Halley Court, Jordan Hill, Oxford OX2 8EJ,
part of Harcourt Education.
Raintree is a registered trademark of Harcourt
Education Ltd.

Editorial: Melanie Copland, Kate Buckingham
and Lucy Beevor
Design: Jo Malivoire and AMR
Picture Research: Mica Brancic
Production: Duncan Gilbert
Originated by Modern Age
Printed and bound in China by South China
Printing Company

10 digit ISBN 1 844 21238 6 (hardback)
13 digit ISBN 978 1 844 21238 5 (hardback)
09 08 07 06 05
10 9 8 7 6 5 4 3 2 1

10 digit ISBN 1 844 21244 0 (paperback)
13 digit ISBN 978 1 844 21244 6 (paperback)
10 09 08 07 06
10 9 8 7 6 5 4 3 2 1

British Library Cataloguing in Publication Data
Thomas, Isabel
Drawing – (Action Art)
741
A full catalogue record for this book is available
from the British Library

Acknowledgements
Corbis pp. **5, 6, 17, 19**; Getty Images pp. **14**
(Stone), **18** (Taxi); Harcourt Education pp. **4, 7,
8, 9, 10, 11, 12, 13, 15, 16, 20, 21, 22, 23, 24**
(Tudor Photography)

Cover photograph of colour pencils reproduced
with permission of Getty (ThinkStock)

Every effort has been made to contact copyright
holders of any material reproduced in this book.
Any omissions will be rectified in subsequent
printings if notice is given to the publishers.

The paper used to print this book comes from
sustainable resources.

Some words are shown in bold, **like this**. You can find them in the glossary on page 23.

A person who makes art is called an artist.

You can be an artist too!

What kinds of art can I do?

There are lots of ways to create art.

You can paint and draw colourful pictures.

sculpture

You can make patterns, prints, and collage.

Sculpting is another kind of art.

What is drawing?

A drawing is a picture of something.

Drawings are made up of lines and shapes.

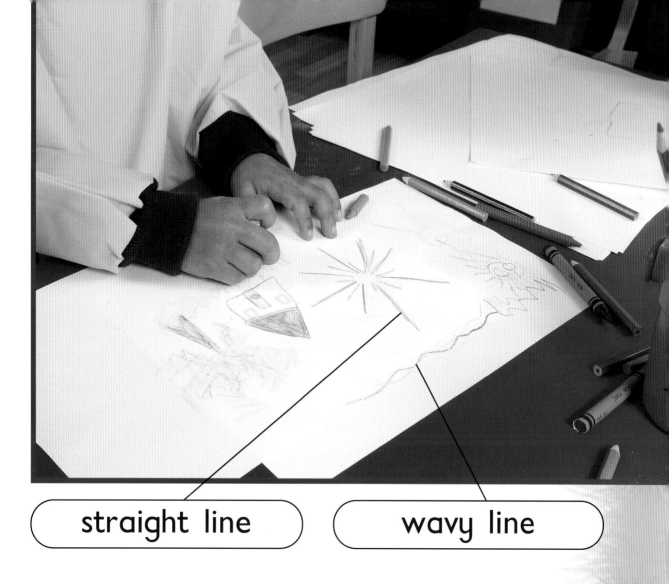

straight line wavy line

This drawing has wavy lines and straight lines.

What shapes can you see?

What can I draw with?

pencil

felt tip pen

crayon

chalk

You can draw with all these **tools**.

They come in many colours.

Pencils and pens make thin lines.

Crayons and chalk make thick lines.

What can I draw on?

You can draw on paper.

Paper comes in lots of different colours and **textures**.

You can draw on card, too.

Try drawing birthday cards for your friends.

What can I draw?

You can draw anything that you can see.

Draw a picture of an animal or your family.

You can draw around a shape.

Try drawing around your hand.

What else can I draw?

Sometimes you draw things that you **imagine**.

These children are drawing funny monsters!

Think about your favourite story.

Try to draw what you are thinking.

How does drawing make me feel?

Drawing is fun.

It can make you feel happy.

When you **display** your drawings, you feel proud.

Let's draw!

Let's draw a **portrait**!

1. Look at one of your friends. First, draw the shape of their head.

2. Now add the hair. Is it long or short? Is it straight or curly?

3. Draw the eyes, nose, and mouth. Look carefully at what shapes they are. Make sure you put them in the right place.

4. Now try to draw a picture of your own face!

Quiz

All of these **tools** can be used for drawing.

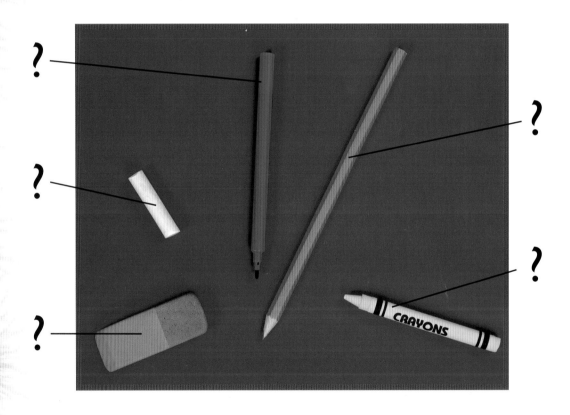

Can you remember their names?

Look for the answers on page 24.

Glossary

 **creative** making something using your own ideas and how you feel inside

 **display** put your art where people can look at it

 **imagine** make things up in your head

 **portrait** picture of somebody

 **texture** how something feels when you touch it

 **tools** the things you use to make art, like pencils and crayons

Index

artist 5

birthday cards 13

chalk 10, 11, 22

collage 7

crayons 10, 11, 22

creative 4

display 19

feeling happy 18–19

imagine things 16–17

kinds of art 6–7

lines and shapes 8–9, 11, 15, 20

paper and card 12–13

pencils and pens 10, 11, 22

pictures 6, 8, 14, 20–21

portrait 20–21

sculpting 7

tools 10, 22

what art is 4

what drawing is 8–9

what to draw 14–17

Answers to quiz on page 22

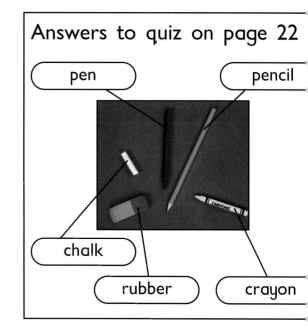

pen

pencil

chalk

rubber

crayon